P9-AOV-440

fabulous brownies

fabulous brownies

Annie Rigg

photography by Laura Edwards

RYLAND
PETERS
& SMALL

LONDON NEW YORK

Senior Designer Iona Hoyle
Senior Editor Céline Hughes
Production Controller Maria Petalidou
Art Director Leslie Harrington
Publishing Director Alison Starling

Prop Stylist Liz Belton
Indexer Hilary Bird

author's acknowledgements

I would like to give enormous chocolate-coated "thank yous" to the wonderful Laura Edwards and Liz Belton for making the pictures in this book so utterly beautiful. And as always, Céline and Iona at Ryland Peters & Small have worked their magic, making everything come together so gorgeously – the dream team.

First published in 2011
by Ryland Peters & Small
20–21 Jockey's Fields
London WC1R 4BW
and 519 Broadway, 5th Floor
New York, NY 10012

www.rylandpeters.com

10 9 8 7 6 5 4 3 2 1

Printed in China

ISBN: 978-1-84975-120-9

Library of Congress Cataloging-in-Publication Data

Rigg, Annie.
Fabulous brownies / Annie Rigg ; photography by Laura Edwards.
p. cm.
Includes index.
ISBN 978-1-84975-120-9
1. Brownies (Cooking) I. Title.
TX771.R558 2011
641.8'653--dc22

2010044807

notes

- All spoon measurements are level unless otherwise specified.
- Eggs used in the recipes in this book are large unless otherwise specified.
- All butter used in the recipes in this book is unsalted.
- Sugar used in the recipes in this book is caster/superfine unless otherwise stated.
- Ovens should be preheated to the specified temperatures. All ovens work slightly differently. We recommend using an oven thermometer and suggest you consult the maker's handbook for any special instructions, particularly if you are cooking in a fan-assisted oven, as you will need to adjust temperatures according to manufacturer's instructions.

For digital editions visit
www.rylandpeters.com/apps.php

contents

just one more square...

Dark, rich, gooey and deeply chocolately, brownies have to be the ultimate chocolate treat. With just a handful of ingredients you can create the most delicious, indulgent squares. Here's a collection of recipes to take these chocolate-loaded bites to the next level and beyond.

Baking cakes can require an electric mixer or maybe a selection of specialized bakeware – not so with brownies. A rectangular or square pan, five or six ingredients and no more than about 40 minutes of your precious time and voilà! Baking a simple tray of brownies requires no technical skill, rigorous beating or mixing – it's a simple case of melting and stirring. And the end result is so scrumptious and decadent that it's near impossible to have just one little piece.

As with all baking, it pays to use the very best ingredients: good unsalted butter, the purest vanilla extract, the freshest eggs and let's not forget the chocolate. I prefer to use chocolate with a medium amount of cocoa solids, around 68%. Feel free to use a higher percentage if that's to your taste, but you may need to increase the sugar slightly to balance the flavours. Why not experiment with chocolate that has bits and pieces added to it, like praline, or more unusual aromatic flavours, from spices to orange oil.

Start with the basic recipe on page 10, and from there the world is your brownie oyster. Chocolate can be paired with all sorts of ingredients: nuts of almost any type can be added to the mixture; and for a more sophisticated, and strictly adult, taste, try soaking dried fruit in alcohol before adding to the cake mixture, e.g. dried cherries with cherry brandy, raisins with sweet sherry and apricots with Marsala. Caramel and chocolate, in my mind, are a marriage made in sugary heaven. Whether it be ultra-sweet dulce de leche, salted caramel or crumbly fudge, all can be folded or swirled in, or scattered on top of a brownie.

There's a fabulous selection of ideas in this book for decorating your brownies to make them super special. Children especially will love the Brownie Pops and Brown(ie) Owls, but why stop there – there's no end to the animal shapes you can make. Try making teddy bear faces, cats or even hedgehogs; all you need is a variety of chocolate drops and sprinkles and an ounce of imagination.

Brownies will keep for three or four days in an airtight box if you don't manage to eat the whole lot in one sitting – and are the perfect treat to tuck into a picnic hamper, pack into boxes as gifts or (occasionally!) pop into a lunchbox.

Brownies can be dressed up or down; cut into large chunks or bite-size morsels; served warm as a dessert with the best (or better still, homemade) ice cream; or cut into tiny squares after dinner in place of a storebought box of chocolates. Above all, they should be as irresistible to behold as they are to taste.

the icing on the cake

There's no denying it, brownies are utterly scrumptious just as they are, freshly baked and cut into squares.

But with a small selection of piping nozzles/tips and a handful of sprinkles, chocolate chips and candies, you'll soon be on the road to some really dazzling chocolate treats. Keep tubs of vanilla fudge pieces, nuts and mini-marshmallows for whenever the need arises for some really special brownies to brighten up a rainy day. I find assorted star-shaped nozzles/tips the most simple and useful when I want to decorate cakes with frosting. You don't need any special skills to pipe rosettes and swirls, just a little practice.

white chocolate buttercream

100 g/3½ oz. white chocolate, chopped
½ teaspoon vanilla extract
100 g/7 tablespoons soft butter
150 g/1 cup icing/confectioners' sugar, sifted

Tip the chocolate into a heatproof bowl set over a saucepan of barely simmering water. Do not let the bottom of the bowl touch the water. Leave until melted and smooth, then leave to cool slightly. In a separate bowl, beat together the butter and sugar until pale and light. Add the vanilla extract and melted chocolate and beat until smooth.

milk chocolate frosting

125 g/4 oz. dark/bittersweet chocolate, finely chopped (I prefer to use a chocolate with a lower cocoa percentage, around 54–68%, for this frosting)
125 g/4 oz. milk chocolate, finely chopped
175 ml/⅔ cup double/heavy cream
1 tablespoon maple syrup or golden syrup
125 g/1 stick soft butter, diced

Tip the chocolates into a small, heatproof bowl. Heat the cream and syrup in a small saucepan until only just boiling. Pour it over the chopped chocolates, add the butter and leave to melt. Stir until smooth, then leave to thicken slightly before using.

chocolate ganache

150 g/5 oz. dark/bittersweet chocolate, finely chopped
150 ml/⅔ cup double/heavy cream
1 tablespoon light muscovado/light brown sugar
a pinch of salt

Tip the chocolate into a small, heatproof bowl. Heat the cream and sugar in a small saucepan until the sugar has dissolved and the cream is just boiling. Add the salt. Pour it over over the chopped chocolate and leave to melt. Stir until smooth, then leave to cool and thicken slightly before using.

chocolate glaze

100 g/3½ oz. dark/bittersweet chocolate, finely chopped
75 g/2½ oz. milk chocolate, finely chopped
1 tablespoon sunflower oil
½–1 tablespoon golden syrup/light corn syrup

Tip all the ingredients into a heatproof bowl set over a saucepan of barely simmering water. Do not let the bottom of the bowl touch the water. Stir occasionally until the chocolate has melted and the glaze is smooth. Remove from the heat and leave to cool and thicken slightly before using.

simple

These are brownies in their most simple but decadent form and several of the recipes in this book start from this basic mixture.

deep dark chocolate

225 g/8 oz. dark/bittersweet chocolate, chopped
150 g/10 tablespoons butter, diced
125 g/½ cup plus 1 tablespoon sugar
125 g/½ cup plus 1 tablespoon light muscovado/light brown sugar
4 eggs, lightly beaten
1 teaspoon vanilla extract
125 g/1 cup plain/all-purpose flour
a pinch of salt

a 23-cm/9-inch square baking pan, greased and lined with greased baking parchment

makes 16 squares

Preheat the oven to 170°C (325°F) Gas 3.

Put the chocolate and butter in a heatproof bowl set over a saucepan of barely simmering water. Stir until smooth and thoroughly combined. Leave to cool slightly.

Add both the sugars and mix well. Add the eggs one at a time, beating well after each addition. Stir in the vanilla extract. Sift the flour and salt into the bowl and stir until smooth.

Pour the mixture into the prepared baking pan, spread level and bake on the middle shelf of the preheated oven for about 20–25 minutes, or until the brownies are set and have a light crust on top.

Remove from the oven and leave to cool completely in the pan before removing from the pan and cutting into 16 squares to serve.

Baked in a muffin pan and filled and topped with vanilla fudge, these cute mini-brownies benefit from being made with the best crumbly fudge you can find.

fudge crumble

175 g/6 oz. dark/bittersweet chocolate, chopped
125 g/1 stick butter, diced, plus extra for greasing
100 g/½ cup sugar
50 g/¼ cup light muscovado/light brown sugar
2 eggs
1 teaspoon vanilla extract
100 g/¾ cup plus 1 tablespoon plain/all-purpose flour, plus extra for dusting
½ teaspoon baking powder
a pinch of salt
50 g/2 oz. vanilla fudge chopped, plus extra to decorate

fudge frosting

125 g/4 oz. dark/bittersweet chocolate, finely chopped
100 ml/⅓ cup double/heavy cream
2–3 tablespoons maple syrup

a 12-cup muffin pan

makes 10

Preheat the oven to 170°C (325°F) Gas 3.

Grease the insides of 10 of the muffin cups and line the base of each with a disc of greased baking parchment. Lightly dust with flour and tip out the excess.

Put the chocolate and butter in a heatproof bowl set over a saucepan of barely simmering water. Stir until smooth and thoroughly combined. Leave to cool slightly.

In a separate bowl, whisk the sugars, eggs and vanilla extract for 2–3 minutes until light and foamy. Add the melted chocolate mixture and stir until combined. Sift the flour, baking powder and salt into the bowl and fold in until well mixed, then stir in the chopped fudge.

Divide the mixture between the prepared muffin cups and bake on the middle shelf of the preheated oven for 15 minutes, or until firm and well risen. Remove from the oven and leave to cool in the pan for 2 minutes, then loosen the edges of each brownie with a small palette knife. Tip the brownies out, upside down, onto a wire rack and leave until completely cold before frosting.

Meanwhile, to make the fudge frosting, put all the ingredients together in a small saucepan over gentle heat. Stir until melted and smooth, then leave to cool and thicken slightly before using. Spoon the frosting over each brownie, allowing it to drizzle down the sides. Scatter with chopped fudge and leave to set before serving.

With swirls of luscious caramel running through them, these brownies are definitely in the grown-up league. Serve warm, as a dessert, with top-notch ice cream.

salted caramel swirl

100 g/1 cup shelled pecans
225 g/8 oz. dark/bittersweet chocolate, chopped
150 g/1 stick plus 2 tablespoons butter, diced
225 g/1 cup sugar
4 eggs, lightly beaten
1 teaspoon vanilla extract
125 g/1 cup plain/all-purpose flour
a pinch of salt

salted caramel

50 g/¼ cup caster/superfine sugar
50 g/¼ cup light muscovado/light brown sugar
2 tablespoons butter
75 ml/⅓ cup double/heavy cream
½ teaspoon sea salt flakes

a 23-cm/9-inch square baking pan, greased and lined with greased baking parchment

makes 25 squares

Make the salted caramel first. Put the caster/superfine sugar and 2 tablespoons water in a small saucepan over low heat and let the sugar dissolve completely. Bring to the boil, then cook until the syrup turns to an amber-coloured caramel. Remove from the heat and add the muscovado/brown sugar, butter and cream. Stir to dissolve, then return to the low heat and simmer for 3–4 minutes until the caramel has thickened and will coat the back of a spoon. Remove from the heat, add the salt, pour into a bowl and leave until completely cold and thick.

Preheat the oven to 170°C (325°F) Gas 3.

Tip the pecans onto a baking sheet and lightly toast in the preheated oven for 5 minutes. Roughly chop and leave to cool. Leave the oven on for the brownies.

Put the chocolate and butter in a heatproof bowl set over a saucepan of barely simmering water. Stir until smooth and thoroughly combined. Leave to cool slightly.

In a separate bowl, whisk the sugar, eggs and vanilla extract. Add the melted chocolate mixture and stir until combined. Sift the flour and salt into the bowl and fold in until well incorporated, then stir in the pecans.

Pour half the mixture into the prepared baking pan and spread level. Drizzle half the salted caramel over the top, then pour the remaining mixture over that. Finish by drizzling the remaining salted caramel on top, then use a round-bladed knife to swirl the mixtures together. Tap the pan on the work surface to level the mixture and bake on the middle shelf of the preheated oven for 20–25 minutes.

Remove from the oven and leave to cool completely in the pan before removing from the pan and cutting into 25 squares to serve.

Peanut butter and jam are a common sandwich filling, but take away the bread, add some chocolate, swirl it all together and it's a new brownie classic.

peanut butter & jam

125 g/4 oz. dark/bittersweet chocolate, chopped
100 g/7 tablespoons butter, diced
175 g/¾ cup plus 1 tablespoon sugar
3 eggs
100 g/¾ cup plus 1 tablespoon plain/all-purpose flour
a pinch of salt
4 generous tablespoons raspberry jam

peanut butter swirl

75 g/⅓ cup cream cheese
1 egg, lightly beaten
1 teaspoon vanilla extract
100 g/½ cup sugar
150 g/⅔ cup peanut butter

a 20 x 30-cm/8 x 12-inch baking pan, greased and lined with greased baking parchment

makes 16–20 portions

Preheat the oven to 170°C (325°F) Gas 3.

Make the peanut butter swirl first. Tip all the ingredients into a bowl and beat until smooth. Set aside.

Put the chocolate and butter in a heatproof bowl set over a saucepan of barely simmering water. Stir until smooth and thoroughly combined. Leave to cool slightly.

In a separate bowl, whisk the sugar and eggs for 2–3 minutes until light and foamy. Add the melted chocolate mixture and stir until combined. Sift the flour and salt into the bowl and fold in until well incorporated.

Spoon two-thirds of the brownie mixture into the prepared baking pan and spread level. Dot one-third of the peanut butter mixture and all of the raspberry jam over the brownie. Spoon over the remaining brownie mixture, then the remaining peanut mixture in equal spoonfuls. Using a round-bladed knife, swirl the mixtures together to create a marbled effect. Tap the pan on the work surface to level the mixture and bake on the middle shelf of the preheated oven for about 20–25 minutes.

Remove from the oven and leave to cool completely in the pan before removing from the pan and cutting into portions to serve.

Buried in the middle of each of these brownie squares is a chocolate-covered caramel, but it could just as well be a peanut butter candy or even a marshmallow.

caramel surprise

1 quantity Deep Dark Chocolate (page 10, up to the stage when the mixture is poured into the baking pan)

25 individual chocolate-covered caramels

a 23-cm/9-inch square baking pan, greased and lined with greased baking parchment

gold foil and ribbon, to gift-wrap (optional)

makes 25 squares

Preheat the oven to 170°C (325°F) Gas 3.

Prepare the Deep Dark Chocolate mixture according to the recipe on page 10, up to the stage when the mixture is poured into the prepared baking pan. Imagine how you will be cutting the baked brownies into 25 squares – in rows and columns of five – then push the chocolate-covered caramels in the middle of what will be each baked brownie square.

Bake on the middle shelf of the preheated oven for 20–25 minutes, or until the brownies are just cooked.

Remove from the oven and leave to cool completely in the pan before removing from the pan and cutting carefully into 25 squares so that there is a caramel in the middle of each square.

If you are gift-wrapping the brownies, cut the gold foil in squares large enough to fit around the brownies and gift-wrap each one neatly. Cut short lengths of ribbon and tie around the gold packages.

These brownies can't decide whether they want to be a dessert or a teatime treat. They're luscious, creamy and dense – so I guess they'd be perfect at any time of day.

marbled cheesecake

200 g/6½ oz. dark/bittersweet chocolate, chopped
150 g/10 tablespoons butter, diced
200 g/1 cup sugar
3 eggs
125 g/1 cup plain/all-purpose flour
a pinch of salt

cheesecake mixture

350 g/1½ cups cream cheese
1 teaspoon vanilla extract
125 g/⅔ cup sugar
2 eggs, lightly beaten

a 20 x 30-cm/8 x 12-inch baking pan, greased and lined with greased baking parchment

makes 16–20 portions

Preheat the oven to 170°C (325°F) Gas 3.

Make the cheesecake mixture first. Tip all the ingredients into a bowl and beat until smooth. Set aside.

Put the chocolate and butter in a heatproof bowl set over a saucepan of barely simmering water. Stir until smooth and thoroughly combined. Leave to cool slightly.

In a separate bowl, whisk the sugar and eggs with a balloon whisk for 1–2 minutes. Add the melted chocolate mixture and stir until combined. Sift the flour and salt into the bowl and fold in until well incorporated.

Spoon three-quarters of the brownie mixture into the prepared baking pan and spread level. Spoon the cheesecake mixture evenly over the top, then dollop the remaining brownie mixture in spoonfuls over that. Using a round-bladed knife, swirl the mixtures together to create a marbled effect. Tap the pan on the work surface to level the mixture and bake on the middle shelf of the preheated oven for about 30–35 minutes, or until just set in the middle.

Remove from the oven and leave to cool completely in the pan before removing from the pan and cutting into portions to serve.

Try adding extra interest to these sweet blondies with dried cranberries or a tablespoon of desiccated coconut and swap the pecans for any nut that takes your fancy.

white chocolate & pecan blondies

75 g/¾ cup shelled pecans
75 g/2½ oz. white chocolate, chopped
175 g/1½ cups plain/all-purpose flour
1 teaspoon baking powder
2 tablespoons malted milk powder
a pinch of salt
125 g/1 stick soft butter
175 g/¾ cup plus 2 tablespoons unrefined sugar
2 eggs, lightly beaten
1 teaspoon vanilla extract
75 g/½ cup white chocolate chips

a 20-cm/8-inch square baking pan, greased and lined with greased baking parchment

makes 16 squares

Preheat the oven to 170°C (325°F) Gas 3.

Tip the pecans onto a baking sheet and lightly toast in the preheated oven for 5 minutes. Roughly chop and leave to cool. Leave the oven on for the brownies.

Melt the chocolate either in a heatproof bowl set over a saucepan of barely simmering water or in the microwave on a low setting.

Sift together the flour, baking powder, milk powder and salt.

In a separate bowl, cream together the butter and sugar until pale and light. Gradually add the eggs, beating well after each addition. Stir in the vanilla extract. Add the melted chocolate and stir until combined. Fold the sifted dry ingredients into the bowl until well incorporated, then stir in the chocolate chips and pecans.

Spoon the mixture into the prepared baking pan, spread level and bake on the middle shelf of the preheated oven for 25–30 minutes, or until the brownies are golden and just cooked.

Remove from the oven and leave to cool completely in the pan before removing from the pan and cutting into 16 squares to serve.

pretty

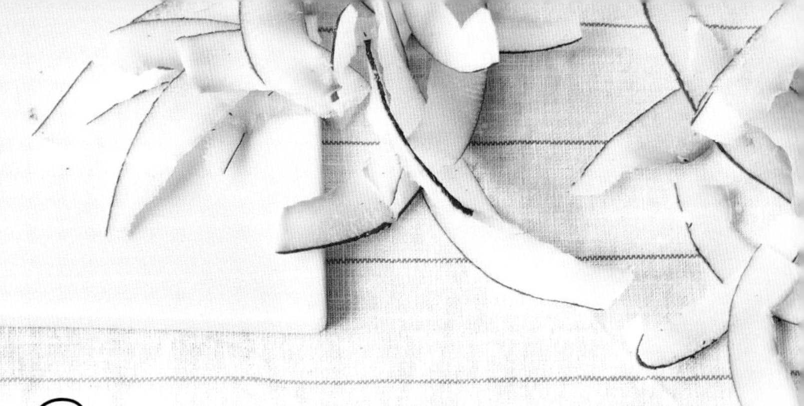

cherry & coconut

200 g/6½ oz. dark/bittersweet chocolate, chopped
125 g/1 stick butter, diced
200 g/1 cup sugar
4 eggs
75 g/⅔ cup plain/all-purpose flour
a pinch of salt
75 g/2½ oz. natural glacé cherries, roughly chopped
50 g/½ cup dried sour cherries, roughly chopped
50 g/⅔ cup desiccated coconut

to decorate

1 quantity Chocolate Ganache (page 9)
fresh coconut shavings, toasted
16 fresh cherries, stems intact

a 23-cm/9-inch square baking pan, greased and lined with greased baking parchment

makes 16 squares

Dried cherries, coconut and rich chocolate are a marriage made in choccy heaven. Top each square with toasted fresh coconut shavings and the finest cherries.

Preheat the oven to 170°C (325°F) Gas 3.

Put the chocolate and butter in a heatproof bowl set over a saucepan of barely simmering water. Stir until smooth and thoroughly combined. Leave to cool slightly.

In a separate bowl, lightly whisk the sugar and eggs with a balloon whisk for 1–2 minutes. Add the melted chocolate mixture and stir until combined. Sift the flour and salt into the bowl and fold in until well incorporated, then stir in the glacé cherries, sour cherries and coconut.

Pour the mixture into the prepared baking pan, spread level and bake on the middle shelf of the preheated oven for about 20–25 minutes.

Remove from the oven and leave to cool completely in the pan. Meanwhile, prepare the Chocolate Ganache according to the recipe on page 9.

Cut the cold brownies into 16 squares. Spread a tablespoonful of Chocolate Ganache over each square and top with coconut shavings and a fresh cherry.

Cut these into bite-size squares, top with a swirl of rich ganache and serve after dinner with coffee in place of the usual box of chocolate truffles.

petits fours

50 g/½ cup dried sour cherries, roughly chopped, or raisins
2 tablespoons brandy, sweet sherry (PX) or Marsala
125 g/4 oz. dark/bittersweet chocolate, chopped
75 g/5 tablespoons butter, diced
125 g/½ cup plus 2 tablespoons sugar
2 eggs
½ teaspoon vanilla extract
50 g/⅓ cup plain/all-purpose flour
a pinch of salt

to decorate

½ quantity Chocolate Ganache (page 9)
crystallized roses and violets, candied ginger, candied orange peel, silver and gold dragees

a 17-cm/6½-inch square baking pan, greased and lined with greased baking parchment

a piping bag, fitted with a star nozzle/tip

makes 25–36

Tip the cherries into a small saucepan, add the brandy and warm gently over low heat. Remove from the heat and leave to cool and soak for 15 minutes.

Preheat the oven to 170°C (325°F) Gas 3.

Put the chocolate and butter in a heatproof bowl set over a saucepan of barely simmering water. Stir until smooth and thoroughly combined. Leave to cool slightly.

Put the sugar and eggs in a mixing bowl and whisk until thick and pale. Add the vanilla and the cherries with any remaining brandy. Sift the flour and salt into the bowl and fold in until well incorporated.

Pour the mixture into the prepared baking pan, spread level and bake on the middle shelf of the preheated oven for about 15 minutes.

Remove from the oven and leave to cool completely in the pan, then refrigerate, still in the pan, until the brownies are firm.

Meanwhile, prepare the Chocolate Ganache according to the recipe on page 9 and spoon into the prepared piping bag.

Tip the firm brownies out of the pan onto a board and cut into about 25–36 cubes. Pipe Chocolate Ganache rosettes on top of each cube. Top with your choice of decoration and refrigerate until ready to serve.

I often think that fresh apricots taste better when they're cooked, and when they're cooked on top of brownies, the whole package really is something else.

apricot & almond

225 g/8 oz. dark/bittersweet chocolate, chopped
150 g/10 tablespoons butter, diced
125 g/1 cup slivered almonds
225 g/1 cup plus 2 tablespoons sugar
4 eggs
1 teaspoon vanilla extract
125 g/1 cup plain/all-purpose flour
a pinch of salt
8 fresh apricots, pitted and quartered

a 20 x 30-cm/8 x 12-inch baking pan, greased and lined with greased baking parchment

makes 16–20 portions

Preheat the oven to 170°C (325°F) Gas 3.

Put the chocolate and butter in a heatproof bowl set over a saucepan of barely simmering water. Stir until smooth and thoroughly combined. Leave to cool slightly.

Meanwhile, put two-thirds of the slivered almonds in a frying pan over low heat and dry-fry, stirring often, until toasted and golden.

In a separate bowl, lightly beat the sugar, eggs and vanilla extract. Add the melted chocolate mixture and stir until combined. Sift the flour and salt into the bowl and fold in until well incorporated, then stir in the toasted almonds.

Pour the mixture into the prepared baking pan, spread level and arrange the quartered apricots on top. Scatter the remaining slivered almonds all over the brownies. Bake on the middle shelf of the preheated oven for 40 minutes, or until the brownies have set and the apricots are soft.

Remove from the oven and leave to cool completely in the pan before removing from the pan and cutting into portions to serve.

Make the white chocolate hearts in advance and refrigerate until needed. Look for heart-shaped sugar sprinkles in bakeware stores or from online suppliers.

love hearts

1 tablespoon butter, melted
1 tablespoon plain/all-purpose flour
1 quantity Deep Dark Chocolate (page 10)

to decorate

150 g/5½ oz. white chocolate, chopped
1 quantity Chocolate Ganache (page 9)
3–4 tablespoons apricot or raspberry jam
red liquid food colouring
red or pink edible glitter
red heart-shaped sugar sprinkles

a baking sheet, lined with baking parchment

12 heart-shaped baking pans measuring 10 cm/4 inches across, baselined with baking parchment (if you don't have as many as 12 pans, just bake the hearts in batches)

a clean toothbrush

small heart-shaped cookie cutters in various sizes

makes 12

Start by making the white chocolate hearts, to decorate. Melt the white chocolate either in a heatproof bowl set over a saucepan of barely simmering water or in the microwave on a low setting. Pour the chocolate onto the prepared baking sheet and spread evenly to a thickness of 2 mm/1⁄16 inch. Leave in a cool place to set completely.

Preheat the oven to 170°C (325°F) Gas 3.

Lightly brush the insides of the heart-shaped pans with the melted butter and line the bases with a piece of greased baking parchment. Now dust the insides of the pans with the flour and tip out the excess.

Prepare the Deep Dark Chocolate mixture according to the recipe on page 10 and divide between the prepared baking pans. (If you don't have 12 pans, you will need to bake the hearts in batches.) Arrange on a baking sheet and cook on the middle shelf of the preheated oven for about 12–15 minutes.

Remove from the oven and leave to cool in the pans for 10 minutes before turning out onto a wire rack to cool completely.

Meanwhile, prepare the Chocolate Ganache according to the recipe on page 9. Warm the jam in a small saucepan, sieve it, then brush it over the tops of the brownies. Leave to set for 5 minutes.

Trickle a little red food colouring onto a saucer, then dip the clean toothbrush into it. Flick the bristles over half the slab of set white chocolate so that it is flecked with red. Sprinkle edible glitter over the remainder of the chocolate and leave to dry, then stamp out hearts with the cookie cutters.

Spread the Chocolate Ganache over the tops of the brownies and decorate with the white chocolate hearts and sugar sprinkles.

A sophisticated little square, chock-full of sweet raspberries and white chocolate, perfect to serve at a summer afternoon tea party.

white chocolate & raspberry

75 g/2½ oz. white chocolate, chopped, plus extra, shaved, to decorate
75 g/⅔ cup plain/all-purpose flour
50 g/⅓ cup ground almonds
½ teaspoon baking powder
a pinch of salt
75 g/5 tablespoons soft butter
150 g/¾ cup sugar
2 eggs, lightly beaten
1 teaspoon vanilla extract
grated zest of ½ unwaxed lemon
50 g/⅓ cup white chocolate chips
150 g/1¼ cups raspberries, plus extra to decorate
1 generous tablespoon slivered almonds

a 20-cm/8-inch square baking pan, greased and lined with greased baking parchment

makes 16 squares

Preheat the oven to 170°C (325°F) Gas 3.

Melt the chocolate either in a heatproof bowl set over a saucepan of barely simmering water or in the microwave on a low setting.

Sift together the flour, ground almonds, baking powder and salt.

In a separate bowl, cream together the butter and sugar until pale and light. Gradually add the eggs, beating well after each addition. Stir in the vanilla extract and lemon zest. Add the melted chocolate and stir until combined. Fold the sifted dry ingredients into the bowl until well incorporated, then stir in the chocolate chips.

Spoon the mixture into the prepared baking pan, spread level and arrange the raspberries evenly over the top. Scatter the slivered almonds over the raspberries. Bake on the middle shelf of the preheated oven for 25–30 minutes, or until golden.

Remove from the oven and leave to cool completely in the pan before removing from the pan and cutting into 16 squares. Decorate with more raspberries and shavings of white chocolate.

coffee blondies

100 g/1 cup shelled pecans
200 g/1 cup light muscovado/ light brown sugar
175 g/1½ sticks butter
3 tablespoons instant coffee granules
2 eggs, lightly beaten
250 g/2 cups plain/ all-purpose flour
2 teaspoons baking powder
a pinch of salt
100 g/⅔ cup dark/bittersweet chocolate chips

to decorate

200 ml/¾ cup double/ heavy cream
2 tablespoons icing/ confectioners' sugar
mixed chocolate shavings
chocolate-coated coffee beans

a 20 x 30-cm/8 x 12-inch baking pan, greased and lined with greased baking parchment

makes 16–20 portions

Use a vegetable peeler to make piles of chocolate shavings for decorating these cappuccino-like squares.

Preheat the oven to 170°C (325°F) Gas 3.

Tip the pecans onto a baking sheet and lightly toast in the preheated oven for 5 minutes. Roughly chop and leave to cool. Leave the oven on for the brownies.

Tip the muscovado/brown sugar and butter into a medium saucepan over low-medium heat and melt, stirring constantly. In a small bowl, dissolve the coffee granules in 1½ tablespoons boiling water. Stir two-thirds into the pan (reserve the rest for the frosting). Remove from the heat, transfer the mixture to a bowl and leave to cool completely.

Stir the eggs and vanilla extract into the pan until smooth. Sift the flour, baking powder and salt into the pan and fold in until well mixed, then stir in the chocolate chips and pecans. Pour the mixture into the prepared baking pan, spread level and bake on the middle shelf of the preheated oven for about 25 minutes, or until just set in the middle and the top has formed a light crust. Remove from the oven and leave to cool completely in the pan. To decorate, whip the cream with the reserved coffee and sugar. Remove the brownies from the pan, cut into portions, top with a dollop of coffee cream and scatter chocolate shavings and coffee beans over the top.

These are a cross between blondies and brownies, with toffee, chocolate chips, nuts and caramel frosting. If you can make spun sugar for decoration, all the better.

butterscotch

75 g/¾ cup shelled pecans
225 g/1¾ cups plain/all-purpose flour
1 teaspoon baking powder
½ teaspoon bicarbonate of/baking soda
a pinch of salt
150 g/10 tablespoons soft butter
150 g/¾ cup light brown (soft) sugar
100 g/½ cup unrefined sugar
2 eggs, lightly beaten
1 teaspoon vanilla extract
50 g/⅓ cup chocolate chips
75 g/2½ oz. toffees, chopped

to decorate

150 g/¾ cup sugar
150 ml/⅔ cup double/heavy cream
200 g/1 stick plus 5 tablespoons soft butter

a 20 x 30-cm/8 x 12-inch baking pan, greased and lined with greased baking parchment

a piping bag, fitted with a plain nozzle/tip

makes 16–20 portions

Preheat the oven to 170°C (325°F) Gas 3.

Tip the pecans onto a baking sheet and lightly toast in the preheated oven for 5 minutes. Roughly chop and leave to cool.

Sift together the flour, baking powder, bicarbonate of/baking soda and salt.

In a separate bowl, cream together the butter and sugars until pale and light. Gradually add the eggs, beating well after each addition. Stir in the vanilla extract. Fold the sifted dry ingredients into the bowl until well incorporated, then stir in the chocolate chips, pecans and toffees. Spoon the mixture into the prepared baking pan, spread level and bake on the middle shelf of the preheated oven for 25 minutes.

Remove from the oven and leave to cool completely in the pan.

To decorate, put the sugar and 1 tablespoon water in a small, heavy-based saucepan over low–medium heat and let the sugar dissolve without stirring. Raise the heat and continue to cook until the sugar turns a deep amber colour. Remove from the heat and add the cream – the caramel will bubble furiously and harden, but stir to melt the caramel into the cream and leave until completely cold.

Beat the butter until light and fluffy, then add the cold caramel in a steady stream and stir until thoroughly incorporated and smooth.

Remove the brownies from the pan and cut into portions. Spoon the caramel frosting into the prepared piping bag and pipe a generous swirl on top of each brownie.

Topped with a mountainous mix of sugary delights – marshmallows, nuts, cherries and chocolate chips – here's a combination that's not for the faint-hearted.

rocky roadies

1 quantity Deep Dark Chocolate (page 10)
75 g/1½ cups mini-marshmallows
75 g/⅔ cup chopped walnuts or pecans
100 g/3½ oz. glacé cherries (natural and/or dyed), chopped
100 g/3½ oz. dark/bittersweet chocolate chips
sugar sprinkles

a 20 x 30-cm/8 x 12-inch baking pan, greased and lined with greased baking parchment

makes 16–20 portions

Preheat the oven to 170°C (325°F) Gas 3.

Prepare the Deep Dark Chocolate mixture according to the recipe on page 10, but bake on the middle shelf of the preheated oven for just 20 minutes.

Remove from the oven and, working quickly, scatter the marshmallows, nuts, cherries, chocolate chips and sugar sprinkles evenly over the top.

Return the brownies to the oven for a further 3 minutes, or until the marshmallows and chocolate chips are just starting to melt. Remove from the oven and leave to cool completely in the pan before cutting into portions to serve.

Looking somewhat like a lunar landscape, these squares should be generously topped with whichever chocolatey malted milk treats take your fancy.

malted milk

75 g/¾ cup shelled walnuts
175 g/1½ cups plain/all-purpose flour
¼ teaspoon baking powder
¼ teaspoon bicarbonate of/baking soda
2 generous tablespoons malted milk powder
a pinch of salt
175 g/1½ sticks soft butter
225 g/1 cup light brown (soft) sugar
3 eggs, lightly beaten
2 teaspoons vanilla extract
75 g/2½ oz. milk-chocolate-coated malted milk balls, halved

to decorate

1 quantity Milk Chocolate Frosting (page 9)
milk- and white-chocolate-coated malted milk balls
assorted chocolate sprinkles

a 23-cm/9-inch square baking pan, greased and lined with greased baking parchment

makes 16 squares

Preheat the oven to 170°C (325°F) Gas 3.

Tip the walnuts onto a baking sheet and lightly toast in the preheated oven for 5 minutes. Roughly chop and leave to cool. Leave the oven on for the brownies.

Sift together the flour, baking powder, bicarbonate of/baking soda, milk powder and salt.

In a separate bowl, cream together the butter and sugar until pale and light. Gradually add the eggs, beating well after each addition. Stir in the vanilla extract.

Fold the sifted dry ingredients into the bowl until well incorporated, then stir in the halved malted milk balls and walnuts.

Spoon the mixture into the prepared baking pan, spread level and bake on the middle shelf of the preheated oven for 20–25 minutes, or until well risen and golden brown.

Remove from the oven and leave to cool completely in the pan.

Meanwhile, prepare the Milk Chocolate Frosting according to the recipe on page 9. Remove the cold brownie from the pan. Spread the Milk Chocolate Frosting evenly over it, then cut into 16 squares. Decorate with malted milk balls and chocolate sprinkles.

If you don't want to make praline for these brownies, make the base recipe with chocolate that has praline pieces already added to it.

hazelnut praline

1 quantity Deep Dark Chocolate (page 10, but make the praline below before you prepare the brownies)

praline

150 g/¾ cup sugar
100 g/⅔ cup blanched hazelnuts

to decorate

1 quantity Chocolate Ganache (page 9)
100 g/½ cup sugar
100 g/⅔ cup blanched hazelnuts, lightly toasted

a baking sheet, lightly oiled with sunflower oil

a 20-cm/8-inch square baking pan, greased and lined with greased baking parchment

makes 12–16

Make the praline first before you start the brownies. Put the sugar and 1 tablespoon water in a small, heavy-based saucepan over low heat and let the sugar dissolve without stirring. Raise the heat and continue to cook for about 2–4 minutes until the sugar turns a deep amber colour. Quickly tip the hazelnuts into the pan and stir to coat evenly in the caramel. Spoon the mixture out onto the oiled baking sheet and leave to cool completely. When cold, whizz in a food processor until finely chopped. Re-oil the baking sheet and set aside.

Preheat the oven to 170°C (325°F) Gas 3.

Prepare the Deep Dark Chocolate mixture according to the recipe on page 10, but fold half of the chopped praline into the mixture. Spoon the mixture into the prepared baking pan, spread level and bake on the middle shelf of the preheated oven for 20–25 minutes.

Remove from the oven and leave to cool completely in the pan. To decorate, prepare the Chocolate Ganache according to the recipe on page 9, then stir in 2 tablespoons of the chopped praline. Refrigerate until thick enough to spread.

Put the sugar and 1 tablespoon water in a small, heavy-based saucepan over low heat and let the sugar dissolve completely. Bring to the boil, then cook until the syrup turns to an amber-coloured caramel. Remove from the heat and plunge the bottom of the pan into a sink of cold water. Quickly tip the hazelnuts into the pan and stir to coat evenly in the caramel. Using a fork, remove the hazelnuts from the caramel so that the caramel leaves long tails and place the nuts on the oiled baking sheet. Leave to harden.

Cut the brownies into diamonds or squares and spread the Chocolate Ganache on each one. Top with some caramelized hazelnuts and serve with ice cream and leftover praline scattered over the top.

German chocolate cake is not German at all but a classic American recipe. The caramel, coconut and pecan frosting sits perfectly on a deep dark brownie.

german chocolate

1 quantity Deep Dark Chocolate (page 10)

to decorate

150 g/1½ cups shelled pecans
150 g/2 cups desiccated coconut
200 ml/¾ cup double/heavy cream
200 g/1 cup light brown (soft) sugar
3 egg yolks
50 g/3 tablespoons butter
1 teaspoon vanilla extract
a pinch of salt
1 quantity Chocolate Ganache (page 9)
edible gold glitter

a 20 x 30-cm/8 x 12-inch baking pan, greased and lined with greased baking parchment

a piping bag, fitted with a star-shaped nozzle/tip

makes 16–20 portions

Preheat the oven to 170°C (325°F) Gas 3.

Tip the pecans onto a baking sheet and lightly toast in the preheated oven for 5 minutes. Roughly chop and leave to cool. Leave the oven on for the brownies.

Put the coconut in a frying pan over low heat and dry-fry, stirring often, until toasted and lightly golden.

Prepare the Deep Dark Chocolate mixture according to the recipe on page 10, but bake on the middle shelf of the preheated oven for just 20 minutes.

Remove from the oven and leave to cool completely in the pan.

To decorate, put the cream, sugar, egg yolks and butter in a medium, heavy-based saucepan over low–medium heat. Cook, stirring constantly, for about 7 minutes, or until the mixture is smooth and has thickened. Remove from the heat and stir in the vanilla extract, salt, and the toasted pecans and coconut. Spread the caramel frosting over the cold brownies. Leave to cool and set for at least 2 hours.

Prepare the Chocolate Ganache according to the recipe on page 9.

Cut the brownies into 16–20 portions. Spoon the Chocolate Ganache into the prepared piping bag and pipe rosettes on top of each brownie square, then sprinkle edible gold glitter over the top.

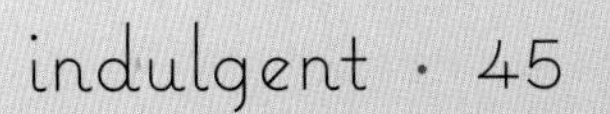

These warmly spiced brownies taste even better if you make them a day or two before you plan to serve them – you just have to be patient!

gingerbread

275 g/9½ oz. dark/bittersweet chocolate, chopped
175 g/1½ sticks butter, diced
125 g/1 cup plain/all-purpose flour
1 teaspoon ground cinnamon
2 teaspoons ground ginger
¼ teaspoon ground nutmeg
a pinch of hot chilli powder
a pinch of salt
50 g/2 oz. crystallized ginger
175 g/¾ cup plus 1 tablespoon dark muscovado/dark brown sugar
2 tablespoons golden syrup or light corn syrup
1 tablespoon molasses
4 eggs
50 g/½ cup slivered almonds, chopped
1 quantity Chocolate Ganache (page 9)
edible gold sprinkles

a 20-cm/8-inch square baking pan, greased and lined with greased baking parchment

makes 16 squares

Preheat the oven to 170°C (325°F) Gas 3.

Put the chocolate and butter in a heatproof bowl set over a saucepan of barely simmering water. Stir until smooth and thoroughly combined. Leave to cool slightly.

Sift together the flour, all the spices and the salt.

Finely chop the crystallized ginger. Lightly whisk the sugar, syrup, molasses, eggs and vanilla extract until combined. Add the melted chocolate mixture and stir until combined. Stir the almonds and half the chopped ginger into the bowl. Fold in the sifted dry ingredients.

Pour the mixture into the prepared baking pan, spread level and bake on the middle shelf of the preheated oven for about 25 minutes, or until the brownies are set.

Remove from the oven and leave to cool completely in the pan. When cold, remove the brownies from the pan, wrap in clingfilm/plastic wrap and leave overnight before frosting.

The next day, prepare the Chocolate Ganache according to the recipe on page 9. Spread over the top of the brownies, score with the tines of a fork to make a diagonal pattern, then cut into 16 squares. Scatter the rest of the chopped ginger and a few gold sprinkles over the top.

This recipe is an ideal way of using up any leftover off-cuts from making brownie shapes. When I say "leftover", of course I'm only joking – who has "leftover" brownies? So you'll need to make up one batch of Deep Dark Chocolate brownies and one of White Chocolate & Pecan Blondies, cut into small squares. If you are making this for adults, you could add a tablespoon of brandy or rum to the sauce.

brownie fondues

1 quantity Deep Dark Chocolate (page 10)
1 quantity White Chocolate & Pecan Blondies (page 22)
strawberries and marshmallows, to serve

dark fondue

150 g/5½ oz. dark/bittersweet chocolate, finely chopped
1–2 tablespoons maple syrup or golden syrup
200 ml/¾ cup double/heavy cream

white fondue

200 g/7 oz. white chocolate, finely chopped
1 teaspoon vanilla extract
150 ml/⅔ cup double/heavy cream

wooden skewers, to serve

Prepare the Deep Dark Chocolate mixture according to the recipe on page 10, and the White Chocolate & Pecan Blondies according to the recipe on page 22. Or use any leftover brownies.

To make the dark fondue, tip all the ingredients into a small saucepan over low heat. Stir constantly to melt the chocolate, but do not allow it to boil or catch on the bottom of the pan. Remove from the heat and pour into a bowl to serve.

To make the white fondue, tip all the ingredients into a small saucepan over low heat. Stir constantly to melt the chocolate, but do not allow it to boil or catch on the bottom of the pan. Remove from the heat and pour into a separate bowl to serve.

Cut the brownies into small cubes and serve with strawberries and marshmallows for dipping, a few skewers, and the two bowls of warm fondue.

brownie whoppers

These started life as whoopie pies, but somewhere along the way they became more fudgy and rich. Definitely not just for the kids...

75 g/2½ oz. dark/bittersweet chocolate, chopped
75 g/5 tablespoons butter, diced
275 g/2 generous cups plain/all-purpose flour
2 tablespoons cocoa powder
1 teaspoon baking powder
1½ teaspoons bicarbonate of/baking soda
a pinch of salt
125 g/⅔ cup light muscovado/light brown sugar
75 g/⅓ cup sugar
1 egg, lightly beaten
125 ml/cup sour cream, at room temperature
½ quantity White Chocolate Buttercream (page 9)
1 quantity Chocolate Glaze (page 9)
sugar sprinkles

2 large baking sheets, lined with baking parchment

a piping bag, fitted with a star-shaped nozzle/tip

makes 12

Preheat the oven to 170°C (325°F) Gas 3.

Put the chocolate and butter in a heatproof bowl set over a saucepan of barely simmering water. Stir until smooth and thoroughly combined. Leave to cool slightly.

Sift together the flour, cocoa powder, baking powder, bicarbonate of/baking soda and salt. In a large bowl, whisk together the sugars, egg and sour cream. Add the melted chocolate mixture and stir until combined. Finally, fold the sifted dry ingredients and 5 tablespoons boiling water into the bowl until well incorporated. Spoon 24 evenly sized dollops onto the prepared baking sheets, leaving plenty of space between each one. Bake on the middle shelf of the preheated oven for about 10–12 minutes. Leave to cool on the baking sheets for 3 minutes, then transfer to a wire rack until cold.

Prepare the White Chocolate Buttercream and Chocolate Glaze according to the recipes on page 9. Spoon the buttercream into the prepared piping bag. Pipe a generous amount over half of the brownie whoppers. Sandwich with the remaining whoppers.

Spoon the glaze over the tops of the whoppers, decorate with sprinkles and leave to set before serving.

You can let your imagination run wild here and make the most of the huge assortment of sprinkles available. You could even stick birthday candles into each wheel.

brownie wheels

1 quantity Kids' Brownies (page 54)

to decorate

1 quantity Milk Chocolate Frosting (page 9)

½ quantity White Chocolate Buttercream (page 9)

chopped mixed nuts, lightly toasted

assorted sugar sprinkles

chocolate vermicelli/jimmies

white and milk chocolate chips

plain round cookie cutters in various sizes

a piping bag, fitted with your choice of nozzle/tip

makes 16–20

It is easiest to stamp out brownie shapes if the base is prepared and baked the day before you plan to decorate your brownies.

Prepare the Kids' Brownies according to the recipe on page 54 and leave to cool completely in the pan. Cover with clingfilm/plastic wrap and leave to rest overnight, if possible.

The next day, prepare the Milk Chocolate Frosting according to the recipe on page 9 and leave to thicken slightly.

Prepare the White Chocolate Buttercream according to the recipe on page 9.

Remove the brownies from the pan. Using the cookie cutters, stamp out rounds in various sizes. Using a palette knife, spread frosting or buttercream around the sides of the brownie wheels.

Tip the chopped nuts, sugar sprinkles and chocolate vermicelli/jimmies onto separate plates and roll each wheel into one of these so that the sides are evenly coated.

Spoon some frosting or buttercream into the prepared piping bag and pipe decorative patterns and swirls on top of the wheels. Experiment with different nozzles/tips to create pretty rosettes, leaf shapes, peaks and more. Or you can simply use a palette knife to spread the frosting or buttercream over the tops. Arrange chocolate chips around the edges of some of the wheels. Leave the frosting to set before serving.

You could make these cute brownies in a selection of sizes to create a whole family of brown(ie) owls. You'll find that each owl has a slightly different expression!

brown(ie) owls

kids' brownies

100 g/1 cup shelled walnuts or pecans (optional)
200 g/6½ oz. dark/bittersweet chocolate, chopped
175 g/1½ sticks butter, diced
250 g/1¼ cups sugar
4 eggs
1 teaspoon vanilla extract
125 g/1 cup plain/all-purpose flour
2 tablespoons cocoa powder
a pinch of salt
75 g/½ cup milk chocolate chips

to decorate

1 quantity Milk Chocolate Frosting (page 9)
chocolate buttons and chips in various sizes and colours
chocolate-covered caramel

a 20 x 30-cm/8 x 12-inch baking pan, greased and lined with greased baking parchment

a 6–7-cm/2½-inch round cookie cutter

makes 12

Preheat the oven to 170°C (325°F) Gas 3.

To make the kids' brownies, if you're adding nuts, tip them onto a baking sheet and lightly toast in the preheated oven for 5 minutes. Roughly chop and leave to cool. Leave the oven on for the brownies.

Put the chocolate and butter in a heatproof bowl set over a saucepan of barely simmering water. Stir until smooth and thoroughly combined. Leave to cool slightly.

In a separate bowl, whisk the sugar, eggs and vanilla extract with a balloon whisk until pale and thick. Add the melted chocolate mixture and stir until combined. Sift the flour, cocoa powder and salt into the bowl and fold in until well incorporated, then stir in the chocolate chips and nuts (if using). Pour the mixture into the prepared baking pan, spread level and bake on the middle shelf of the preheated oven for 25 minutes.

Remove from the oven and leave to cool completely in the pan.

Meanwhile, prepare the Milk Chocolate Frosting according to the recipe on page 9. Remove the cold brownie from the pan. Using the cookie cutter, stamp out 12 rounds from the brownies and arrange on a board or tray. Using a palette knife, spread the Milk Chocolate Frosting evenly over the top and sides. Slice about one-third off some smaller chocolate buttons and arrange in overlapping rows across the bottom half of each owl. Arrange giant buttons as eyes, then top with white buttons and chocolate chips, sticking them together with a dab of frosting. Cut the chocolate-coated caramel into triangles for the beaks and press onto the owls just below the eyes. Twit twoo.

Keep a lookout for red and white peppermint candies to top these minty brownies. At Christmas time, you could decorate them with striped candy canes.

mint chocolate chip

1 quantity Kids' Brownies (page 54, but see method, opposite)
1 teaspoon peppermint extract
75 g/½ cup white chocolate chips
red and white peppermint candies, to decorate

mint buttercream

225 g/1¾ cups icing/confectioners' sugar
125 g/1 stick soft butter
1 teaspoon peppermint extract

chocolate glaze

125 g/4 oz. dark/bittersweet chocolate, chopped
1 tablespoon golden syrup/light corn syrup

a 23-cm/9-inch square baking pan, greased and lined with greased baking parchment

makes about 16 portions

Preheat the oven to 170°C (325°F) Gas 3.

Prepare the Kids' Brownies according to the recipe on page 54, but swap the vanilla extract for 1 teaspoon peppermint extract and add 75 g/½ cup white chocolate chips to the mixture at the same time as the milk chocolate chips and nuts (if using).

Spoon the mixture into the prepared baking pan, spread level and bake on the middle shelf of the preheated oven for about 25 minutes, or until the top has formed a light crust.

Remove from the oven and leave to cool completely in the pan.

Meanwhile, to make the mint buttercream, sift the icing/confectioners' sugar into a mixing bowl, add the soft butter and beat until smooth, pale and light. Add the peppermint extract and mix until combined.

Remove the cold brownie from the pan. Spread the buttercream in an even layer over the top and refrigerate until firm.

To make the chocolate glaze, put the chocolate and syrup in a heatproof bowl set over a saucepan of barely simmering water. Do not let the bottom of the bowl touch the water. Stir occasionally until the chocolate has melted and the glaze is smooth. Remove from the heat and leave to cool and thicken slightly before using.

Spread the glaze over the top of the mint buttercream and refrigerate until set.

Cut the brownies into portions using a long, hot knife (this will ensure the knife glides neatly through the glaze and buttercream). Decorate with red and white peppermint candies.

These aren't strictly cupcakes or brownies. They are, however, fudgy and dark, and the perfect option when you want brownies but in cute, individual portions.

cupcake brownies

175 g/6 oz. dark/bittersweet chocolate, chopped
125 g/1 stick butter, diced
150 g/¾ cup light brown (soft) sugar
2 eggs
1 teaspoon vanilla extract
100 g/¾ cup plus 1 tablespoon plain/all-purpose flour
¼ teaspoon baking powder
a pinch of salt
1 quantity Milk Chocolate Frosting (page 9)
sugar sprinkles

a 12-cup muffin pan, lined with 10 pretty cupcake cases

a piping bag, fitted with a star-shaped nozzle/tip

makes 10

Preheat the oven to 170°C (325°F) Gas 3.

Put the chocolate and butter in a heatproof bowl set over a saucepan of barely simmering water. Stir until smooth and thoroughly combined. Leave to cool slightly.

In a separate bowl, whisk the sugar, eggs and vanilla extract for 2–3 minutes until light and foamy. Add the melted chocolate mixture and stir until combined. Sift the flour, baking powder and salt into the bowl and fold in until well incorporated.

Divide the mixture between the prepared cupcake cases, filling them two-thirds full. Bake on the middle shelf of the preheated oven for 15 minutes, or until firm and well risen.

Remove from the oven and leave to cool in the pan for 2 minutes, then transfer the cupcakes to a wire rack to cool completely.

Meanwhile, prepare the Milk Chocolate Frosting according to the recipe on page 9 and spoon into the prepared piping bag. Pipe a generous swirl over each cupcake brownie. Scatter sugar sprinkles over the top and leave to set before serving.

If you can't decide whether to bake brownies or cookies, why not make both? Here, the two mixtures are combined to make one big cookie – or is it a brownie?

brookies

cookie dough

125 g/1 cup plain/all-purpose flour
½ teaspoon bicarbonate of/baking soda
a pinch of salt
100 g/7 tablespoons soft butter
100 g/½ cup light brown (soft) sugar
50 g/¼ cup sugar
1 egg, lightly beaten
1 teaspoon vanilla extract
75 g/½ cup dark/bittersweet chocolate chips

brownie mixture

125 g/4 oz. dark/bittersweet chocolate, chopped
75 g/5 tablespoons butter, diced
125 g/⅔ cup sugar
2 eggs
1 teaspoon vanilla extract
60 g/½ cup plain/all-purpose flour
a pinch of salt
50 g/½ cup chopped pecans

10 round baking pans, 10 cm/4 inches in diameter and 3 cm/1 inch deep, greased and baselined with baking parchment

makes 10

Preheat the oven to 170°C (325°F) Gas 3.

Make the cookie dough first. Sift together the flour, bicarbonate of/baking soda and salt. In a separate bowl, cream together the butter and sugars until pale and light. Gradually add the egg, beating well after each addition. Stir in the vanilla extract. Fold the sifted dry ingredients into the bowl until well incorporated, then stir in the chocolate chips. Cover and refrigerate for 30 minutes.

Now make the brownie mixture. Put the chocolate and butter in a heatproof bowl set over a saucepan of barely simmering water. Stir until smooth and thoroughly combined. Leave to cool slightly.

In a separate bowl, whisk the sugar, eggs and vanilla extract until pale and doubled in volume. Add the melted chocolate mixture and stir until combined. Sift the flour and salt into the bowl and fold in until well incorporated, then stir in the pecans.

Divide the brownie mixture between the prepared baking pans and spread level. Using a spoon, roughly dollop the cookie dough on top of the brownie mixture.

Place the pans on a baking sheet and bake on the middle shelf of the preheated oven for about 15 minutes, or until the cookie dough is golden brown.

Remove from the oven and leave to cool in the pans for 5 minutes, then loosen the edges of each brookie with a small palette knife. Tip the brookies out onto a wire rack and leave to cool completely.

I have decorated these pops with festive sprinkles, but there's no reason why you couldn't make them Valentine-themed with heart decorations and cutters.

brownie pops

1 quantity Kids' Brownies (page 54)

3–4 tablespoons apricot or raspberry jam

to decorate

1 quantity Milk Chocolate Frosting (page 9)

assorted sugar sprinkles, stars and other edible festive decorations

a 20 x 30-cm/8 x 12-inch baking pan, greased and lined with greased baking parchment

a 5-cm/2-inch round cookie cutter

24 wooden lolly/pop sticks

makes 24

It is easiest to stamp out brownie shapes if the base is prepared and baked the day before you plan to decorate your brownies.

Preheat the oven to 170°C (325°F) Gas 3.

Prepare the Kids' Brownies according to the recipe on page 54.

Remove from the oven and leave to cool completely in the pan.

Remove the cold brownie from the pan. Using the cookie cutter, stamp out 24 rounds from the brownies and arrange on a board or tray.

Warm the jam in a small saucepan, sieve it, then brush it all over the brownie rounds. Leave on a wire rack for 5–10 minutes to set.

Meanwhile, prepare the Milk Chocolate Frosting according to the recipe on page 9 and leave to thicken slightly.

Using a palette knife, spread the Milk Chocolate Frosting evenly all over the brownie rounds, then push a lolly/pop stick into each pop. Lay them on a sheet of baking parchment and leave until the frosting is starting to set. Decorate with an assortment of sprinkles and festive decorations by making patterns on the faces of the pops and by scattering sprinkles generously over the edges.

index

useful suppliers of bakeware & edible cake decorations

UK

www.cakescookiesandcraftsshop.co.uk

www.jane-asher.co.uk

www.lakeland.co.uk

www.makeawishcakeshop.co.uk

www.mycookshop.com

www.squires-shop.com

www.thecookskitchen.com

US

www.confectioneryhouse.com

www.crateandbarrel.com

www.kitchenkrafts.com

www.sugarcraft.com

www.surlatable.com

www.williams-sonoma.com

www.wilton.com